A+ books

Animal Opposites

Long
and
Short

An Animal Opposites Book

by Lisa Bullard

consulting editor: Gail Saunders-Smith, PhD
content consultant: Zoological Society of San Diego

Capstone press

Mankato, Minnesota

Some animals grow longer than a minivan.
Others are shorter than a jelly bean.
Let's learn about long and short
by looking at animals around the world.

Long

Pythons are the
world's longest reptiles.
Some stretch more than
30 feet.

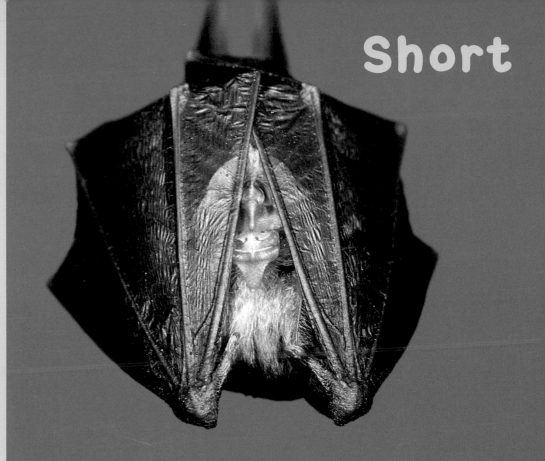

Short

Horseshoe bats are some of
the world's shortest mammals.
They're about the size
of a person's big toe.

Long

Look up, up, up
to see the top of
a giraffe's long neck.

Short

Meerkats have short necks.
They sit up to look out
for other animals.

Long

A chameleon's tongue
is longer than its body.

A chameleon uses its
sticky tongue to catch
flies to eat.

Short

Flies have short bodies. They are just the right size for a chameleon to snack on.

Long

Moray eels are fish
with long skinny bodies.

Moray eels hide in rocks
or coral reefs. They jump out
at tasty fish swimming by.

Fire gobies are short fish.
They are shy and like to hide.

Long

Walkingsticks are
the world's longest insects.
They look like twigs.

Some walkingsticks grow
more than a foot long.

Ladybugs are short
but easy to see.
They are brightly colored.

Long

Fire salamanders have bright marks on their long bodies. The marks are a sign that fire salamanders taste bad.

Strawberry arrow frogs
are short but deadly.
Their skin is poisonous.

Long

Elephants have long noses
called trunks.

16

Gorillas have short noses
to sniff for jungle food.

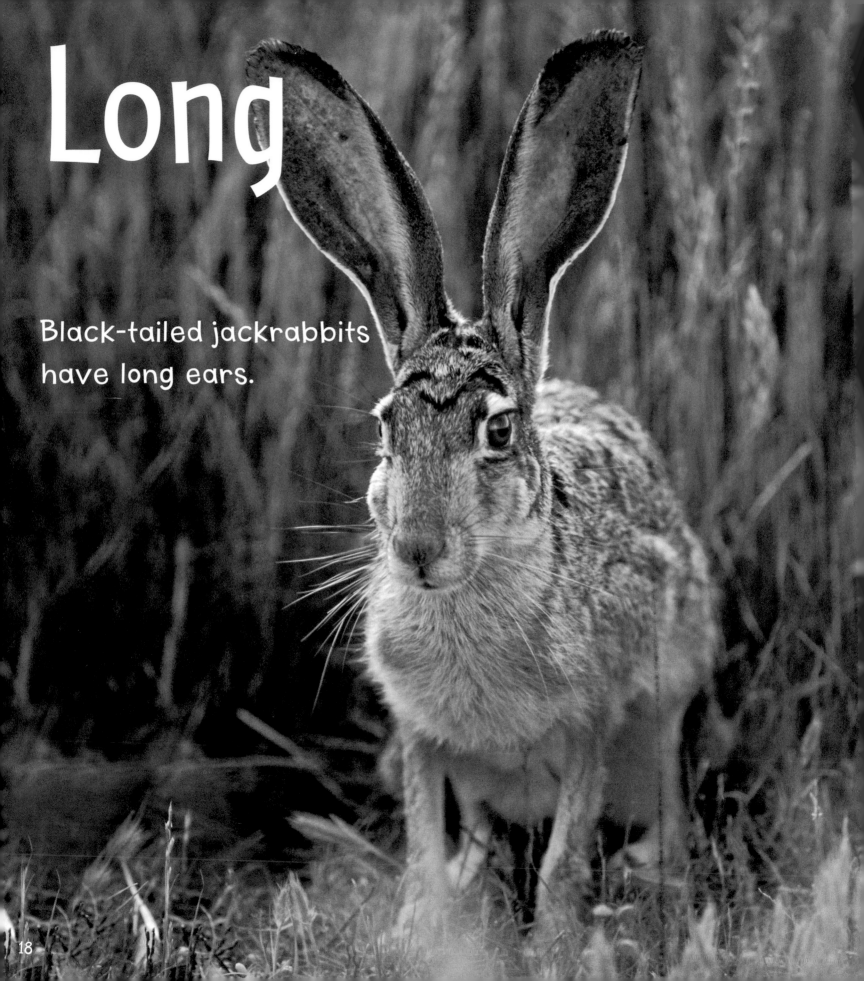

Long

Black-tailed jackrabbits have long ears.

Groundhogs have short ears.

Some groundhogs are also called woodchucks, marmots, and whistle pigs.

Long

Ring-tailed lemurs have long furry tails.

Mandrills have short stubby tails.

Long

Long skinny ferrets are part of the weasel family.

Short

Lemmings are short animals
that some weasels eat.

Long

Flamingos use their long legs to wade for food.

Short

Penguins waddle from place to place with their short legs.

Some long animals swim in the sea.
Others stomp across the land.
Some short animals fly through the air.
Others dig tunnels underground.

What kinds of long and short animals live near you?

Did You Know?

An elephant's trunk has more than 40,000 muscles. Elephants use their trunks to breathe, smell, reach, grab, drink, wrestle, and even shower.

Flamingos sleep standing on one of their long legs.

When a giraffe can't reach a leaf to eat, it sticks out its tongue. A giraffe's tongue is about as long as a child's arm.

Penguins are the only birds that can swim but can't fly. They use their short legs to steer underwater.

At almost 25 inches, a lemur's tail is longer than its whole body.

Glossary

burrow (BUR-oh)—a hole in the ground where an animal lives

coral reef (KOR-uhl REEF)—an area of coral skeletons and rocks in shallow ocean water

insect (IN-sekt)—a small animal with a hard outer shell, six legs, three body sections, and two antennas; most insects have wings.

mammal (MAM-uhl)—a warm-blooded animal that has a backbone and feeds milk to its young; mammals also have hair and give live birth to their young.

poisonous (POI-zuhn-uss)—able to harm or kill with poison or venom

reptile (REP-tile)—a cold-blooded animal that breathes air and has a backbone; most reptiles lay eggs and have scaly skin.

wade (WAYD)—to walk through water

Read More

Deegan, Kim. *My First Book of Opposites.*
New York: Bloomsbury Children's Books, 2002.

Doudna, Kelly. *Long and Short.* Opposites.
Edina, Minn.: Abdo, 2000.

Jenkins, Steve. *Actual Size.* Boston: Houghton
Mifflin, 2004.

Whitehouse, Patricia. *Zoo Sizes.* Zoo Math.
Chicago: Heinemann, 2002.

Internet Sites

FactHound offers a safe, fun way to find Internet sites related to this book.
All of the sites on FactHound have been researched by our staff.

Here's how:

1. Visit *www.facthound.com*
2. Type in this special code **0736842756**
   for age-appropriate sites. Or enter a
   search word related to this book for
   a more general search.
3. Click on the **Fetch It** button.

FactHound will fetch the best sites for you!

Index

A+ Books are published by Capstone Press,
151 Good Counsel Drive, P.O. Box 669, Mankato, Minnesota 56002.
www.capstonepress.com

1 2 3 4 5 6 10 09 08 07 06 05

Library of Congress Cataloging-in-Publication Data
Bullard, Lisa.
Long and short: an animal opposites book / by Lisa Bullard.
    p. cm.—(A+ books. Animal opposites)
    Includes bibliographical references (p. 31) and index.
    ISBN 0-7368-4275-6 (hardcover)
    1. Animals—Miscellanea—Juvenile literature. 2. Size perception—Miscellanea—Juvenile
literature. I. Title. II. Series.
QL49.B7749 2006
590—dc22   2005000634

Summary: Brief text introduces the concepts of long and short, comparing some of the world's
    longest animals with animals that are short.

Credits
Donald Lemke, editor; Kia Adams, designer; Kelly Garvin, photo researcher;
    Scott Thoms, photo editor

Photo Credits
Brand X Pictures, 26 (giraffe); Bruce Coleman Inc./Hans Reinhard, 4, 14; Bruce Coleman
Inc./John Shaw, cover (penguin), 7; Corbis/David A. Northcott, 15; Corbis/Jeff Vanuga,
22; Corbis/Naturfoto Honal, 24; Corbis/Stephen Frink, 11; Corel, 27 (groundhog);
Creatas, 1 (penguin), 2 (penguin), 3 (frog); Digital Vision Ltd., 1 (gorilla), 2 (elephants),
3 (gorilla), 26 (eel), 27 (meerkats); Dwight R. Kuhn, 9; Gail Shumway, 13; Getty Images
Inc./Anup Shah, cover (giraffe); Getty Images Inc./Art Wolfe, 20; Getty Images
Inc./Eastcott Momatiuk, 25; James P. Rowan, 12; Minden Pictures/Foto Natura/Hugo
Willocx, 5; Minden Pictures/Gerry Ellis, 16; Nature Picture Library/Bengt Lundberg, 23;
Peter Arnold Inc./Martin Harvey, 21; Photodisc, 1 (giraffe), 6; Photodisc/G.K. & Vikki
Hart, 3 (ferret); Seapics.com/Masa Ushioda, 10; Tom & Pat Leeson, 18; Tom Stack &
Associates Inc./Erwin and Peggy Bauer, 19; Tom Stack & Associates Inc./Kitchin & Hurst,
8; Tom Stack & Associates Inc./Thomas Kitchin, 17

Note to Parents, Teachers, and Librarians

This Animal Opposites book uses full-color photographs and a nonfiction format to
introduce children to the concepts of long and short. *Long and Short* is designed
to be read aloud to a pre-reader or to be read independently by an early reader.
Photographs help listeners and early readers understand the text and concepts
discussed. The book encourages further learning by including the following sections:
Did You Know?, Glossary, Read More, Internet Sites, and Index. Early readers may
need assistance using these features.